TRADITIONAL MOHAWK CEREMONIES

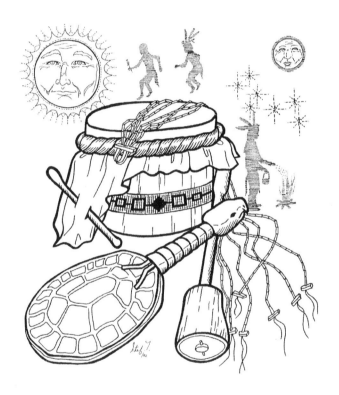

Product of the
Native North American Travelling College

Copyright © 2017 by The Native North American Travelling College

Traditional Mohawk Ceremonies

Traditional Ceremonies

Throughout the year Mohawk people gather to give thanks for the constant return of gifts the Creator has put here for us. Certain events take place at almost every ceremony. The first being the Thanksgiving Address - Ohen:tonkarihwatehkwen - which is recited at the beginning and end of every ceremony. It is an acknowledgement and thanksgiving to all creation. First to the people who have gathered, then Mother Earth, the waters of the world, the fish life, the Three Sisters, plants, medicines, berries, animals, trees, birds, the Four Winds, Our Eldest Brother the Sun, Grandmother Moon, the Stars, the Thunders, the Four Sacred Beings and the Creator.

CREDITS

Artist - Stephanie Thompson
Research - Jayne George
Typesetting & Layout - Becky Bero
Cover - Dave Fadden

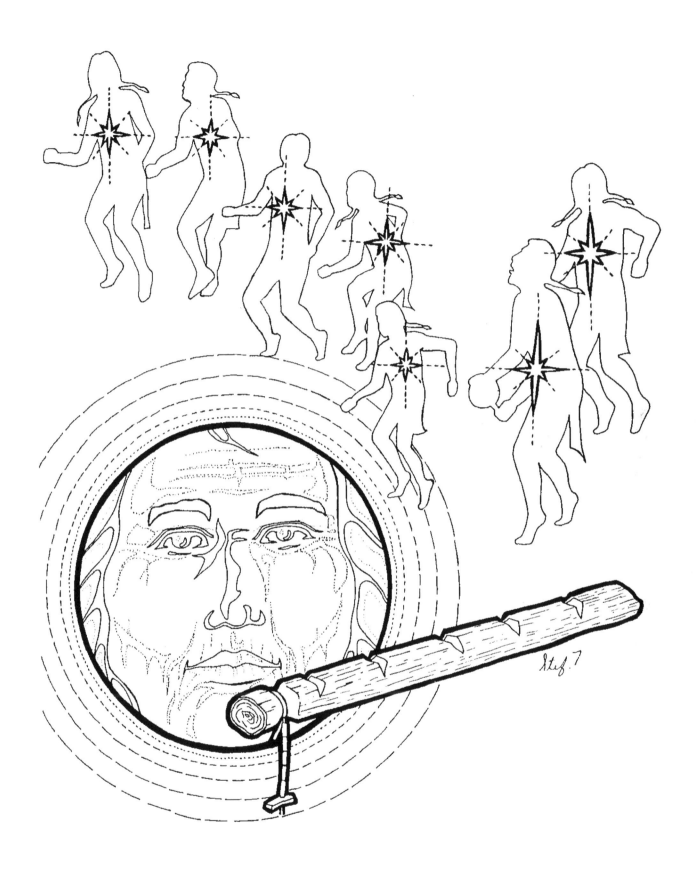

The start of the Midwinter ceremonies is determined by when the Big Dipper is directly above. Then the people will wait for the first new moon, sleep five nights, and the next day will begin the Midwinter ceremonies.

The First day of Midwinnter is Sha'tekohsehra
Stirring of the Ashes
The first day of Midwinter is called the Stirring of the Ashes (Jan.-Feb.). The symbolism of this is that the ashes turn to dirt and dirt is the flesh of Mother Earth. The ashes are stirred to revive life.

Second day of Midwinter Ohstonwa'ko:wa -
Great Feather Dance

The first Great Feather Dance is sponsored by the Faithkeepers to the Creator. The second Great Feather Dance is sponsored by the Chiefs, Clanmothers, and the people. The third Great Feather Dance is sponsored by all the people for the Creator only.

Third day of Midwinter is Wa'therara:ken
White Basket Sacrifice

A fancy, pure white basket is made and used to hold tobacco. An elder recites on behalf of all the people. He gives a report of the past year's activities and asks the Creator and all life forms to be supportive for the coming year. After this is done the basket will be put into the fire as an offering.

Fourth day of Midwinter is Aton:wa
Personal Thanksgiving Chant and Name Confirmation

A man walks to the four directions of the Longhouse. He reminds the Faithkeepers, the Chiefs, Clanmothers, the people, and then the children of their duties. The man then thanks each group and praises them.

This is also the day when men will sing their personal thanksgiving song. They address the Creator and all life forms to thank and praise them and to request that they be of assistance in the coming year.

Name Confirmation
Babies of all clans get their names raised and confirmed.

Fifth day of Midwinter is Oneho:ron
Drum Dance
A song and dance is done. The water drum is used. A spiritual history about the beginning of the world and the people is recited. This is the people's thanksgiving through dance and speech.

Sixth and last day of Midwinter is Kaientowa:nen
Peach Stone Game
It is said to be a game that the Creator enjoys most. Clans play against clans. The people put in their favorite possessions. A Singer may put in his favorite water drum or rattle. A basketmaker may put in her favorite basket. Someone who sews may put in their favorite traditional style outfit.

Hato:wi Ceremony
Medicine Mask Society (Jan.-Feb.)
The Hato:wi help to heal people when they are sick. One must be a member of the society in order to participate. The Hato:wi are our grandfathers.

Enatihsehsta:ta

Tobacco Burning for Sap Collectors (Feb. - Mar.)

This ceremony is done a few days before the maple trees are tapped. The people request that the Creator and the four sacred Sky-Dwellers protect them and prevent the large limbs of the maple trees from falling on them while they gather the sap.

Wahta
Maple Tree Ceremony (Feb.- Mar.)
Upon receiving their drink of maple sap the people stand up and thank the Creator for their good health and good fortune. They give thanks to all of the trees through the maple tree.

Ohki:weh

Dead Feast or ghost Dance (Mid March)

At this time the people will gather together with the spirit of relatives who have passed on. We will sing, dance, and feast with our deceased.

Ratiwe:ras

Thunder Dance (April, sometime May) 1 day

When winter is over, after hearing thunder for the first time, a day is set for the Thunder Dance. This ceremony is done to thank the Thunderers for returning to replenish the waters in the rivers, ponds, lakes, and oceans.

Ka:nen

Planting or Seed Ceremony (May) 1 day

The people bring different kinds of seeds. The Peach Stone game is played between the men and women to determine who will do the planting.

Moon Dance (April - May)
Offering thanksgiving to the Moon, who is the leader of all the women.

Ken niionhontesha
Strawberry Festival (Mid June)

After being handed a drink of juice made from strawberries the people stand up to give greetings and thanks to the Creator for being able to see again the fruit of the strawberry. The strawberry juice is called the Great Medicine.

Skanekwen'tara:ne
Raspberry (July)
The raspberry is the leader of the bush berries. This ceremony is generally combined with the Strawberry Festival.

O'rhotsheri
Bean Ceremony (July)
On this day thanks and greetings are given to the Three Sisters, especially the Bean.

Okahsero:ta
Green Corn (Aug.)
A Corn Dance is done in honor of the corn life. Soup is made from white corn before it fully matures.

Kaientho'kwen Enhontekhwaro:roke
First day of Harvest Ceremony
Three Great Feather Dances (Sept., sometimes Oct.)

Second day of Harvest Ceremony

A Tobacco burning takes place to acknowledge the Creator for fulfilling our requests since the time of Mid-winter, and to thank the Creator and all other life forms for supporting the people for what was received up to this time. Round bread is made to symbolize the Sun, Moon, and Stars.

Third day of Harvest Ceremony is Aton:wa
and Name Confirmation

Fourth day of Harvest Ceremony is Kaientowa:nen
The Peach Stone Game is played between the men and women to thank the Creator for the good harvest.

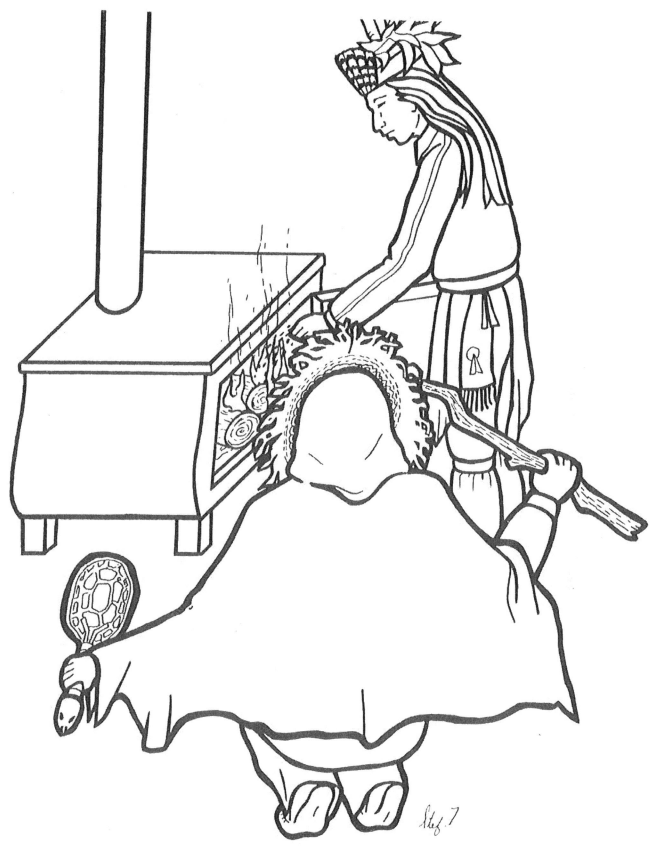

Hato:wi Ceremony
Medicine Mask Society
Similar to the one done after Midwinter.

Ratiwe:ras
Thunder Dance (Oct.)
It is done exactly like the one held in the spring time. This time it is done to say farewell to the Thunderers.

Ohki:weh' (Oct.)
This ceremony is done like the one that took place in the spring. (A feast for all relatives who have passed on).

Ontkenhnhokten
This is End of Seasons (Nov.) 1 day
This the last Ceremony of the year. The people chant their personal songs and give thanks to the
Creator for the entire year.

Marriage

A marriage can take place any time of the year. The bride carries a basket of material or clothing that symbolizes her commitment to mend and keep clean the clothing of her husband and any children they may have. The man carries a basket with a wedding cake made of white corn (corn bread) mixed with strawberries. This symbolizes his acceptance to provide food for his wife and any children they may have. The couple exchange the baskets as a symbol of their commitment to a healthy marriage.

Coloring Book Traditional Ceremonies

Throughout the year Mohawk people gather to give thanks for the constant return of gifts the Creator has put here for us. Certain events take place at almost every ceremony. The first being the Thanksgiving Address **Ohen:tonkarihwatehkwen**- which is recited at the beginning and end of every ceremony. It is an acknowledgement and thanksgiving to all creation. First to the people who have gathered, then Mother Earth, the waters of the world, the fish life, the Three Sisters, plants, medicines, berries, animals trees, birds, the Four Winds, our Eldest Brother the Sun, Grandmother Moon, the Stars, the Thunders, the Four Sacred Beings, and the Creator.

The next event is the Great Feather Dance - **Ohstonwa'ko:wa.** It is the Creator's song and dance. It is to show our gratitude to all life and to energize the entire life forms of the world. The turtle rattle represents Mother Earth and it is used to sing the **Ohstonwa'ko:wo** so all life can become recharged with lifes energy.

A strawberry drink is prepared during each ceremony. It is the leader of all the berry plants and it is a chosen sacred plant. It is called the "Great Medicine" and is a tonic.

Marriage

A marriage can take place any time of the year. The bride carries a basket of material or clothing that symbolizes her commitment to mend and keep Clean the clothing of her husband and any children they may have. The man carries a basket with a wedding cake made of white corn (corn bread) mixed with strawberries. This symbolizes his acceptance to provide food for his wife and any children they may have. The couple exchange the baskets as a symbol of their commitment to a healthy marriage.

The start of Midwinter ceremonies is determined by when the Big Dipper is directly above. Then the people will wait for the first new moon, sleep five nights, and the next day Midwinter ceremonies begin.

The first day of Midwinter is Sha'tekohsehra - Stirring of the Ashes

The first day of Midwinter is called the Stirring of the Ashes (Jan.-Feb.)
The symbolism of this is that the ashes turn to dirt and dirt is the flesh of Mother Earth. The ashes are stirred to revive life.

Second day of Midwinter **Ohston wa'ko:wa** - Great Feather Dance
The first Great Feather Dance is sponsored by the Faithkeepers to the Creator. The second Great Feather Dance is sponsored by the Chiefs, Clanmothers, and the people. The third Great Feather Dance is sponsored by all the people for the Creator only.

Third day of Midwinter is **Wa' therara:ken** - White Basket Sacrifice
A fancy, pure white basket is made and used to hold tobacco. An elder recites on behalf of all the people. He gives a report of the past year's activities and asks the Creator and all life forms to be supportive for the coming year. After this is done the basket will be put into the fire as an offering.

Fourth day of Midwinter is **Aton:wa** - Personal Thanksgiving Chant and Name Confirmation
A man walks to the four directions of the Longhouse. He reminds the Faithkeepers, the Chiefs, Clanmothers, the people, and then the children of their duties. The man then thanks each group and praises them.

This is also the day when every person will sing their personal thanksgiving song. They address the Creator and all life forms to thank and praise them and to request they be of assistance in the coming year.

Name Confirmation (Name Raising)
Babies of all clans get their names raised and confirmed.

Fifth day of Midwinter is **Oneho:ron** - Drum Dance
A song and dance is done. The water drum is used. A spiritual history about the beginning of the world and the people is recited. This is the people's thanksgiving through dance and speech.

Sixth and last day of Midwinter is **Kaientowa:nen** - Peach Stone Game
It is said to be a game that the Creator enjoys most. Clans play against clans. The people put in their favorite possessions. A singer may put in his favorite water drum or rattle. A basketmaker may put in her favorite basket. Someone who sews may put in their favorite traditional style outfit.

Hato:wi Ceremony - Medicine Mask Society (Jan. - Feb.)
The Hato:wi help to heal people when they are sick. One must be a member of the society in order to participate. The Hato:wi are our grandfathers.

Enatihsesta:ta - Tobacco Burning for Sap Collectors (Feb. - March)
This ceremony is done a few days before the maple trees are tapped. The people request that the Creator and the four sacred Sky-Dwellers protect them and prevent the large limbs of the maple trees from falling on them while they gather the sap.

Wahta - Maple Tree Ceremony (Feb. - March)
Upon receiving their drink of maple sap the people stand up and thank the Creator for their good health and good fortune. They give thanks to all of the trees through the maple tree.

Ohki:weh' (Dead Feast or Ghost Dance) (Mid March)
At this time the people will gather together with the spirit of relatives who have passed on. We will sing, dance, and feast with our deceased.

Ratiwe:ras (Our Grandfathers) - Thunder Dance (April, sometimes May) 1 day
When winter is over, after hearing thunder for the first time, a day is set for the Thunder Dance. The ceremony is done to thank the Thunderers for returning and they will work to replenish all the water in the rivers, ponds, lakes, and oceans.

Ka:nen Planting or Seed Ceremony (May) 1 day
The people bring different kinds of seeds. The Peach Stone game is played between the men and women to determine who will do the planting.

Moon Dance (April - May)
This ceremony is done to offer thanksgiving to the Moon, who is the leader of all the women.

Ken niionhontesha Strawberry Festival (Mid June)
After being handed a drink of juice made from strawberries the people stand up to give greetings and thanks to the Creator. The strawberry juice is called the Great Medicine and is considered the leader of the berry world.

Skanekwen'tara:ne Raspberry (July)
The raspberry is the leader of the bush berries. This ceremony is generally combined with the Strawberry Festival.

O'rhotsheri - Bean Ceremony (July)
On this day thanks and greetings are given to the Three Sisters, especially the Bean.

Okahsero:ta - Green Corn (Aug.)

A Corn Dance is done in honor of the corn life. Soup is made from white corn before it fully matures.

Kaientho'kwen Enhontekhwaro:roke

First day of Harvest Ceremony - Three Great Feather Dances (Sept., sometimes Oct.)

Second day of Harvest Ceremony

A Tobacco burning takes place to acknowledge the Creator for fulfilling our requests that began at the Midwinter. To thank the Creator and all other life forms for supporting the people for what was received up to this time. Different sizes of round bread are made to symbolize the Sun, Moon, and Stars.

Third day of Harvest Ceremony **Aton:wa** and Name Confirmation

Fourth day of Harvest Ceremony is **Kaientowa:nen** -The Peach Stone Game is played between the men and women to thank the Creator for the good harvest.

Hato:wi Ceremony - Medicine Mask Society

Similar to the one done after Midwinter.

Ratiwe:ras (Grandfathers) - Thunder Dance (Oct.)

It is done exactly like the one held in the spring time, but this time it is to say thank you and to bid farewell to the Thunderers.

Ohki: weh' (Oct.)

This ceremony is done like the one that took place in the spring. (A feast for all relatives who have passed on).

Ontkenhnhokten This is End of Seasons (Nov.) I day

This the last Ceremony of the year. The people chant their personal songs and give thanks to the Creator for the entire year.

The Native North American Travelling College has been at the forefront of cultural education and revitalization. It was established on the Akwesasne Mohawk Territory in 1974 under the name North American Indian Travelling College by Ernest Kaientaronkwen Benedict and Michael Kanentakeron Mitchell.

The Native North American Travelling College continues to evolve to meet the needs of a changing community. We need more than ever to promote and preserve our language culture and history, not only for our own sake, but to foster a greater appreciation and understanding in the outside community.

1 Ronathahon:ni Lane
Akwesasne, Ontario K6H 5R7

P.O. Box 273
Hogansburg, NY 13655

Tele: 613 932-9452
Fax: 613 932-0092
web: www.nnatc.org

Made in the USA
Monee, IL
20 February 2021